Animal Heroes

By F. R. Robinson

Celebration Press
Pearson Learning Group

Contents

Children and their pets often form strong bonds with each other.

Why Do They Act That Way?

Do you have a pet? If you do, you probably care a lot about it, right? You miss it when you go away. You worry when it's sick. You're excited to see it when you come home. You make sure it's happy and healthy.

Does your pet care about you in a similar way? Most people would answer yes. If you have a dog, it may run to greet you at the door. It may wag its tail. If you have a cat, it may meow and rub against your legs. It might follow you around or lie in your lap.

Dogs and other animals learn to perform tricks because they are given rewards.

Of course, it *seems* as if pets care about us. Yet animal **researchers** aren't so sure.

Scientists agree that animals can learn to act in certain ways. Dogs can learn to come when you call, dolphins can learn to jump out of the water in pairs, and certain kinds of birds can learn to repeat words.

To train an animal, we often reward it for doing what we want. Usually the reward is food or attention and affection.

Some scientists believe that much of what we think of as caring in pets is really an attempt to get a reward. For example, your cat may greet you at the door because it knows you will pet it.

Some scientists also believe that certain animal behaviors people interpret as "caring" may be driven by survival **instincts**. For example, if your dog barks at an intruder, is it trying to protect you? Maybe not. Perhaps the dog barks because it is trying to protect itself or because it is afraid.

Yet in some cases it seems as if pets really do care about their owners. For example, many pet owners describe how their pets act when the owners aren't feeling well. The pets might stay by their side to comfort them, or remain quiet instead of pestering them to play. Do the pets understand their owners are sick? It surely can seem as if they do.

News accounts of animal bravery tell of pets that have saved their owners from fires, **avalanches**, and floods. Some animals have risked their lives to save people or animals they've never met.

Are these animal heroes motivated by feelings of caring? Why else might animals do these things? Think about these questions as you read about some real-life animal heroes.

Dolphins are playful and appear to like being around people.

Dolphins to the Rescue

If you've been to an **aquarium**, you've probably seen dolphins. Dolphins live in most of our oceans and in some rivers, too. They are mammals that travel in groups. They communicate with one another using a wide variety of whistles and clicks.

Dolphins are playful, intelligent animals, and they seem to be interested in people. They also adapt well to life in an aquarium. For these reasons they can easily learn to perform many tricks.

The best-known kind of dolphin, the one that looks as if it's smiling, is the bottle-nosed dolphin. Bottle-nosed dolphins are about 13 feet long and weigh about 600 pounds. Like other mammals, they have lungs and must surface to breathe. They do so through a **blowhole** on the top of their heads.

Dolphins have been seen following boats and ships at sea. They seem to enjoy swimming in the waves that vessels make as they cut through the water. Over many centuries, they have gained a reputation for helping sailors in trouble. In at least one case, dolphins even saved a man from a shark.

It was early evening on July 23, 1996, when people on board the diving boat *Jadran* saw five dolphins swimming near the boat. The boat was cruising in the Gulf of Aqaba, part of the Red Sea between Egypt's Sinai Peninsula and Saudi Arabia.

The captain had stopped the *Jadran* to let the passengers, who had planned to do some diving in the gulf, watch the dolphins playing. Many people enjoy swimming with dolphins, and Martin Richardson, a 29-year-old British tourist, along with two others from the boat decided to join the dolphins for a swim.

The three tourists swam with the dolphins for a short while. Then two of them returned to the *Jadran*. Richardson stayed in the water.

Suddenly his diving companions on the boat heard a terrible scream. They looked toward where the sound had come from and saw Richardson bounding up and out of the water. They could also see blood in the water around him and realized that he was being attacked by a shark.

One of the crew members set off in a small rubber boat to help Richardson, while others on the boat watched. The dolphins had left the area before the attack, but three of them now came back—and it seemed as if they were there to help.

The dolphins swam around Richardson, putting themselves between the man and the shark and smacking the water with their tails and flippers. Dolphins usually exhibit this behavior when they are protecting their young from sharks.

The dolphins continued to circle around Richardson for several minutes, leaping into the air, slapping their fins on the water, and scaring the shark away. Then the small boat reached Richardson, and the crew member dragged him on board.

Dolphins like these saved Martin Richardson's life after the shark attack.

Richardson was bleeding and severely hurt, with deep bites on his back, shoulder, and chest. He was rushed to shore and then to an Egyptian army hospital in El-Tor.

It was clear to everyone that a shark had attacked Richardson. The dolphins, by circling around him, most likely saved his life.

Did the dolphins know they were saving a human? Why would they do that? Scientists disagree on the answers. You'll learn more about what they think later in the book.

Dogs form strong bonds with their owners.

A Dog Hero

Dogs and people have lived together for thousands of years. Dogs are the oldest known **domesticated**, or tamed, animal. Over time, people have bred dogs to help them in many ways. Dogs have been bred to hunt, pull sleds, rescue people, and herd cattle or flocks of sheep. Many dogs were also bred to be watchdogs. Others were bred to be companions, which is what most dogs are today.

Like dolphins, dogs are very smart and easy to train. Dogs can learn to come, to sit and stay, and to do tricks. Dogs can also learn to perform more complex tasks, such as finding drugs hidden in people's luggage and helping visually impaired people get around. We usually train dogs to do these things by rewarding them with treats. But dogs sometimes seem to act on their own, without rewards from their masters.

Gary Watkins, an 11-year-old, was playing outside in the California sunshine one day, chasing lizards. The family dog, Weela, was outside with him. Suddenly Weela charged into Gary and knocked him aside. Gary's mother, Lori, looked on, confused. Weela had always been gentle with Gary.

Weela, an American pit bull terrier similar to the one shown here, saved many people and animals.

Then, quick as lightning, a rattlesnake struck from the path. It bit Weela full in the face. It seemed as though Weela had known that the rattler was about to bite Gary. She pushed the boy away from the snake, putting herself in harm's way.

After many days of suffering, Weela recovered from the snake bite. A rattlesnake bite might have made Gary very sick or even killed him. Did Weela know what she was doing?

It's hard to say. But a few years later, Weela performed more amazing rescue feats. Her actions saved many people and animals. In 1993, because of heavy rains, a dam broke on the nearby Tijuana River, which normally was narrow and shallow. The rushing waters surrounded people's homes and barns. Many people and animals were stranded on rooftops and on small islands of mud. The water flowed around them so quickly that it was too dangerous to try swimming to safety.

Lori Watkins and her cousin Carol Kaspar, along with Weela, started out to rescue a hospitalized friend's animals. According to Lori, Weela seemed to sense where the water was too deep or the currents were too dangerous for them to cross. Weela swam ahead in the flooded area, leading them across in places where they could cross safely. With Weela leading them back and forth, they were able to rescue the animals.

After another week of heavy rain and worse flooding, Lori and Carol discovered several horses and dogs stranded on an island. Again Weela led the way, keeping them away from swift currents and **quicksand**. They were able to get the horses off the island, but the dogs were too scared to let Lori and Carol take them across the water to safety.

Lori thought of a way Weela could help. She strapped a heavy bag of food to Weela's back in a backpack. Then Weela led Lori and Carol through shallow places across the river to put food out for the dogs. They did this again and again, with 65-pound Weela sometimes carrying 50 pounds of food at one time.

Finally, after about a month and many food deliveries, the dogs grew trusting enough for Lori and Carol, guided by Weela, to get them off the island. Without the food Weela delivered, they probably would not have survived.

Weela helped save 30 people, 29 dogs, 13 horses, and 1 cat during about three months of flooding. She won a special award for being so heroic.

Did Weela know she was saving lives? Many scientists would say she did.

Binti Jua from the Brookfield Zoo with her baby, Koola

A Kindly Gorilla?

Gorillas are the largest of the apes. They come from Africa and are **vegetarians**. They eat berries, fruits, flowers, leaves, bark, and roots. Only gorillas in captivity eat meat.

These animals are about as tall as people when they stand on two legs, but they are much wider and heavier. Male gorillas weigh as much as 450 pounds, while females weigh about 200 pounds. They usually walk on all fours, putting their weight on their feet and on the knuckles of their hands.

Gorillas live in close-knit groups, led by an older male. Mountain gorillas spend most of their time on the ground. Lowland gorillas spend more time in trees. At night, gorillas make nests out of twigs and leaves. Baby gorillas stay with their mothers for about three years.

With their large, bony, ridged foreheads and deep-set eyes, gorillas may look mean and fierce to some people. But gorillas are generally shy, gentle animals. They respond well to people and do not hurt them unless they feel threatened or are attacked. Gorillas are also very intelligent. Scientists have even been working with a few gorillas to teach them sign language.

Just how gentle and intelligent are they?

One Friday afternoon a typical crowd of visitors watched the gorillas in the Tropic World exhibit at the Brookfield Zoo in Chicago. One of the gorillas, named Binti Jua, roamed around with her 17-month-old baby, Koola, on her back.

Somehow a three-year-old boy managed to climb over the rail that surrounded the exhibit. The boy fell more than 15 feet into a concrete pit inside the exhibit and landed near seven gorillas. He lay unmoving, apparently unconscious.

Horrified zoo visitors called for help. As the zookeepers rushed to the scene, Binti Jua, with Koola hanging onto her back, lumbered over to the injured boy and picked him up.

Would the gorilla harm the little boy? People feared the worst, but Binti Jua picked up the unconscious child and cradled him gently in her arms.

The Tropic World exhibit at the Brookfield Zoo, where Binti Jua lived with Koola and five other gorillas

Besides Binti Jua and Koola, five other gorillas were in the enclosure. When another gorilla came near, Binti Jua turned away with the boy in her arms.

Witnesses said the gorilla seemed to be trying to protect the little boy. Binti Jua had been specially trained to take care of a baby. When she was a baby, Binti Jua was rejected by her mother and was raised by people. Her keepers wanted to make sure that she would be a good mother to her baby. Did she help the boy because of that experience?

The gorilla carried the boy around a bit and then put him down. But she didn't put him down just anywhere. She put him down in the best possible place—at the doorway where the zookeepers exit and enter. It was as though the gorilla knew it was the exact spot where people would come to get the boy. **Paramedics** were waiting there, and they rushed the child, who had regained consciousness, to the hospital.

Not one of the gorillas harmed the boy. Although he had serious injuries from his fall, he recovered.

Did Binti Jua know she was helping an injured boy? How did the mother gorilla know what to do? Zoo officials say that she acted out of compassion for the hurt child. Some scientists agree, but others believe the act to be just instinct.

Vietnamese potbellied pigs have become popular pets.

Lulu, the Potbellied Pig

Vietnamese potbellied pigs come from Southeast Asia. They get their name from their big potbelly that almost drags along the ground. They have straight tails that they can wag when they are excited, as dogs do. Their skin is usually black, and always very wrinkled. They can weigh 150 pounds and measure 18 inches high at the shoulder.

Vietnamese potbellied pigs used to be raised as a source of food. In the last 100 years, however, they have become popular pets.

The pigs have little hair and don't shed like dogs, so they seldom cause allergies. They are also very smart. As a matter of fact, pigs are thought to be one of the most intelligent animals.

Vietnamese potbellied pigs can be trained in many of the ways dogs are trained. They can be housebroken, can learn to come when called, and are known to be very loyal. For all these reasons many people consider Vietnamese potbellied pigs to be great pets.

But how could a pig save a person's life?

Jo Ann Altsman and her husband, Jack, of Beaver Falls, Pennsylvania, had given their daughter a Vietnamese potbellied pig as a gift, but it seemed their daughter didn't really want it. She asked her parents to pig-sit while she went out of town and never picked her up once she returned. So Jo Ann took in the pig, named LuLu, as her own.

One morning Jo Ann collapsed onto the floor. She had had a heart attack. She was not unconscious, though, and was able to yell for help.

LuLu approached. She looked at Jo Ann and started to cry, Jo Ann reports. Jo Ann says LuLu produced tears and made crying sounds.

LuLu, a Vietnamese potbellied pig, saved her owner by getting a driver's attention.

Next the pig pushed out through the little door the Altsmans had created just for LuLu and the family dog. The door was a little too small for LuLu, and she cut her belly on the way out. Then, even though she had never left the yard on her own before, she somehow managed to push the gate open.

She trotted out to the street. There LuLu waited for cars. When a car came by, she lay down in the street with her legs up in the air.

The first person who drove by was afraid to get out of the car. But the next driver stopped, thinking that the pig was injured and needed help. To his surprise, LuLu got up and led the man to the house to Jo Ann.

The driver telephoned for help. When the paramedics arrived in just a few minutes, LuLu tried to get into the ambulance with Jo Ann. The paramedics shooed her away gently.

Thanks to LuLu, the story had a happy ending. Jo Ann got to the hospital in time and had heart surgery. Doctors say that if only 15 more minutes had passed, she likely would have died.

It seemed as though LuLu knew just what to do to save her master's life. But how could a pig know how to get her master the help she needed? How did she know to stop a car? There does not seem to be a simple answer.

LuLu was rewarded with a jelly donut by Jo Ann. In addition, the American Society for the Prevention of Cruelty to Animals (ASPCA) honored LuLu with a special award for bravery.

Do you think animals are capable of sympathy?

What Do You Think?

What do these stories of extraordinary rescues tell us about animals? It's hard to say for sure. It *seems* these animals were all smart enough to know how to help in an emergency. And they all seemed to care about saving another's life.

Why then do some scientists question this conclusion? Scientists must have proof of something before they can say it's absolutely true. Scientists generally prove their theories by doing experiments. They need to see that a group of animals all respond the same way to the same type of situation.

To prove that an animal is aware of another's feelings or is making conscious decisions is tricky. How can scientists test for sympathy or caring in animals when animals can't explain their feelings? Even if there was a test to measure caring, would a whole group of animals respond the same way to the same situation? Probably not. A group of humans wouldn't.

Some famous scientists, such as Jane Goodall, believe from their research that animals do show feelings. Jeffrey Masson, Marc Bekoff, and a growing number of scientists agree that at times animals show feelings rather than simply acting on instinct.

In any case, the animals in these stories understood that there was a crisis and figured out what to do about it. There are thousands of case histories of animals doing unbelievably heroic acts. We may not know what mental processes they use or have scientific proof to explain their behavior, but we do have evidence—their brave acts. They saved lives. They were all heroes.